The Schiwetz Legacy

1. *April in DeWitt County*

The Schiwetz Legacy

AN ARTIST'S TRIBUTE TO TEXAS, 1910–1971

Pictures by E. M. *(Edward Mueggl)* "Buck" Schiwetz

SELECTED UNDER THE DIRECTION OF JOHN H. LINDSEY

INTRODUCTION BY R. HENDERSON SHUFFLER

NOTES BY THE ARTIST WITH JOHN EDWARD WEEMS

UNIVERSITY OF TEXAS PRESS, AUSTIN AND LONDON

Library of Congress Cataloging in Publication Data

Schiwetz, Edward Muegge, 1898–
    The Schiwetz legacy.

    1. Texas—Description and travel—Views. I. Title.
N6537.S35L5   917.64′04′6   72-1577
ISBN 0-292-77502-4

Dedicated to the memory of

BERTHOLD "TEX" SCHIWETZ

Contents

Plates

13

Acknowledgments

The artist and the publisher wish to express special thanks to the owners of the paintings, drawings, etchings, and lithographs in this book for their kindness in permitting the reproduction of their treasures and for their patience while the process went forward. Ownership of the various pictures is acknowledged individually in the list of plates.

Most of the pictures in this book were included in a retrospective show of the artist's work entitled "Texas' Buck Schiwetz," organized and conducted in San Antonio by the Institute of Texan Cultures of The University of Texas. We are particularly indebted to R. Henderson Shuffler, Executive Director of the Institute, who also wrote the introduction to this book, and to Al Lowman of the Institute's staff, who assisted in choosing and collecting the pictures and who generously made available to John Edward Weems his tape recordings of Buck Schiwetz' remarks about his pictures along with other valuable material.

We are also grateful to J. Wayne Stark, Director of the Memorial Student Center of Texas A&M University, to Richard "Buck" Weirus, Executive Director of the Association of Former Students of Texas A&M University, and to others of Buck Schiwetz' alma mater who assisted materially. Special thanks are also due to the Humble Oil and Refining Company, which introduced so much of Buck Schiwetz' work to the public and which remains interested in his contribution to the Texas heritage.

Our deepest gratitude, however, must go to John H. Lindsey of Houston, businessman, art collector, and long-time friend of Buck Schiwetz, who labored indefatigably in choosing pictures for the show and the book, in obtaining permission from their owners, and in pulling the whole project together. Without his assistance this book would not have been possible.

Introduction

"I hope to leave behind me," Buck Schiwetz once said, "a collection of indigenous paintings which will faithfully portray Texas as it is." In this book you will find proof of his success. It contains selections of his work in many styles and media, done over a period of more than half a century. They depict the full gamut of Texas scenery, wildlife, architecture, back country, towns, and cities, as well as the principal basics of our economy: farming, ranching, agribusiness, oil, chemicals, and petrochemicals. This is a summation of sixty years of ceaseless striving by a competent and sensitive artist to show us the beauties he finds in all things Texan.

"I don't care how desolate, how threadbare, any part of Texas is," he once told an interviewer, "it's beautiful to me." And, seen through the loving eyes of this talented native son—as depicted in his warm and eloquent sketches, watercolors, paintings, lithographs, and etchings—it becomes beautiful for all of us. He brings to the commonplace, often the shoddy, old abandoned houses and mouldering historic landmarks to which he has a special devotion, a beauty, charm, and dignity to be cherished by us all.

This is the result for which Buck strives. He wants us to see and appreciate, as he does, "the indigenous Texas scene, with its multifarious blandishments." Almost single-handedly, he has, over the years, changed our attitudes toward the hidden beauties of our countryside and the honest values of our old buildings. To him, more than any other Texan, belongs credit for the healthy growth of interest in the restoration, preservation, and reconstruction of these relics of our past.

Texas' best-known and best-loved artist is a complex and self-contradictory character of amazing durability and drive. Over the years he has "seen everything twice and done everything half a dozen times," yet, he continues to look on the world with the fresh awareness of a child and to paint with the vigor and speed of an artist in his prime.

In the early 1920's a young, slightly gaunt Buck Schiwetz was making some of the delicately romanticized pencil sketches of San Antonio and Dallas that appear in this book. Several hundred miles away, the now-thriving oil and petrochemical city of Odessa was a dusty little cow town, dozing in the harsh sunlight of the southern tip of the Staked Plains. Neither would know each other for many years to come. Yet, in the devious ways of destiny, Odessa was fated to give Buck his most descriptive and favored latter-day nickname.

Like most small and isolated towns, Odessa in the 1920's had to create its own amusements. Chief of these was following and cheering the town baseball team. When the team made a trip to play on an enemy field, half the town went along. There was one trip each season where everybody went. That was when the team played in Ojinaga, just across the Rio Grande from Presidio.

The combination of a trip "abroad" and a baseball game, all in one hot afternoon, was more than any West Texan could withstand. Add the fact that, in this bone-dry Prohibition era, you could buy all the good Mexican beer you could drink, legally and cheaply, at the Ojinaga combination ballpark-bullring and you had an outing worth dreaming about for months beforehand and recalling with pleasure for months afterward. Then, too, the Ojinagans were a fun-loving hospitable people who viewed baseball as a festive spectacle, rather than a seriously competitive sport. They cheered both sides with equal enthusiasm and impartial good humor.

Star hitter for the Odessa team was a ponderous German, called, quite naturally, "Dutch." He could put his heft behind a swing of the bat and send the ball sailing over the left-field fence, almost at will. Then he would trot doggedly around the bases, while the crowd went wild. The Ojinagans loved him, but not for his prowess with the big stick, alone.

The summers are spectacularly hot and dry in the Presidio-Ojinaga country. Dutch, like most fat men, was very susceptible to the heat. Before the game was well under way, he had shed his shirt and undershirt. When he hit a homer and started jogging around the diamond, the jiggling and bobbling of his topless torso was, to say the least, quite noticeable. This titillating spectacle delighted the Ojinagans. They giggled, nudged each other, pointed, guffawed, and cheered.

"Aleman Titi Grande" was their hero. By this descriptive name he was known for the remainder of his days.

When Buck, in his later years, became ponderously plump, an irreverent friend, recalling the ample Germanic hero of old, applied the name to him. It stuck. Today he signs many of his letters to intimates as "Aleman Titi Grande."

Prolonged personal correspondence with Buck is an educational experience. His stationery bears the return address of the "Half-S Semi-Ranch, Hunt, Texas." His letters are a weird mixture of Hill Country German, florid English, and imaginative grammar, with some of the loveliest malapropisms in both languages you will ever encounter. Each epistle is both a joy and a despair for the recipient. In a letter early this year, for example, he reported: "Aus here ist es extremely kalt—beinabe 5°. For kalt for baden in the South Fork. Es is better that we beiben schmutzig. Stay mit Gesundheit. No sniffels." With the aid of a German-English dictionary and considerable imagination, this translates into a report on the weather and the health of the Schiwetzes.

Yet, when he chooses, Buck can be both coherent and eloquent, as when he wrote about the old Spanish missions: "I am excited by the romantic aura, the rich heritage, the immaculate architecture of our missions. Although I remain awed by San José, its grandeur, the compound layout, adroit handling of ornamentation, and the ingenuity behind the mill water wheel and granary, my favorite remains Concepción . . . its good taste in design—compact purity of architecture."

Aside from the beauty-queen endowments that provided his nickname, the burly artist has the build of a retired wrestler, with an eighteen-inch neck, muscular shoulders and arms, an impressive girth in the lower midsection, and sturdy legs. In the 1930's, when Buck first joined Paul Franke and Joe Wilkinson in founding an advertising firm, their cubbyhole office in the old Cotton Exchange Building was just a few doors from the Houston City Police gym. To keep in shape, the young artist spent many noon hours at the gym, matching grunts, groans, and strangle-holds with stout young policemen. He still swims almost daily, the year around, in the icy waters of the Guadalupe, which flows beside his Hill Country home. He roams the nearby hills, often barefoot, and can walk down most of the younger men of his acquaintance.

Beneath this robust exterior lurks the soul of a poet—sensitive, shy, moody, and gentle. He has a warm affection for all of God's creatures. His capacity for generous and enduring friendship is an ornament to mankind.

Every time Buck sits down to sketch or paint, these days, he murmurs a little prayer: "Please God, just one more —I know I can't do it without you." Raised as an Episcopalian, he works closely with the numerous Baptists at Hunt, with Alcoholics Anonymous, and with all others who fight against alcoholism and drug addiction. His greatest happiness seems to come from trying to help those who are in despair.

He and his wife, Ruby Lee (another gifted and dedicated artist), live as close to Nature as possible. Their Hill Country retreat, near the village of Hunt, consists of a compound of small native-rock buildings on a high bluff above a bend of the Guadalupe River. One of the buildings is a showroom for Buck's latest works, another is a workshop for Ruby Lee. The others are living quarters and guesthouses. Down on the river, suspended just above the cold, clear, rushing water, is a glassed-in studio in which Buck works.

The place is literally overrun by pets. Gentle-hearted Ruby Lee can't turn away a hungry stray, so no less than seventeen cats gather in the little clearing by their house each afternoon at feeding time. Buck, who affects a disdain for the cats, bestows upon them a delightful assortment of ribald names and somehow always seems to be on hand at feeding time to watch the show. He claims as his own an assortment of half-tamed wild things, who slip in shyly from the surrounding brush to share the daily Schiwetz bounty.

One recent Christmas I received from Buck a small, carefully wrapped cardboard box, emblazoned with a cheery "Merry Christmas." Inside, packed in bright bits of colored tissue, were these mementoes of his pets: A small pill bottle containing dried deer droppings, with a hand-scrawled label—"To hell with the Yuletide—Dodie." Around the bottle, secured by a rubber band, was another message—"A slight token from dear departed 'Dodie,' our pet deer. She must be dead all the time now. Oh! She so enjoyed sharing Purina Cat Chow with our wardrobe of 17 felines and 'Stinkie Pie,' the polecat. Have snaps to authenticate this precious scene." And carefully packed into the box, between the bits of tissue, were two Texas buckeye beans, one singed bit of nopal leaf, one spine of tasajillo cactus, one very small sprig of mistletoe, one hackberry leaf and berry, three river cypress sprigs, four sprigs of native cedar, one mesquite leaf, one feather from the redbird "Blush," who had been "devatstated" by "Pearl Gray," the grandmother of the feline horde, one bit of wild turkey feather from the flock they had practically tamed, and four fragments of straw matting that Ruby Lee had used in a manger scene for the holidays until several sheep she had imported for the production broke in and devoured the decorations. Buck's note added, "I say to Hell with sheep! They dissipated my spineless cactus, prized red-and-white honeysuckle, lantana rows—but engendered complete disdain for Johnson grass, which they were purported to obliterate."

And there you have a glimpse of the wondrous private world of Edward Muegge Schiwetz. His public image is very different, though just as genuine. Buck hates all phonies with a passion; he neither poses nor pretends.

He is the scion of an old and a respected Texas family. His great-grandfather, Jacob Schiwetz, landed at Indianola around 1846, one of the thousands of German immigrants to Texas sponsored by the society of noblemen known as the Mainzer Adelsverein. "He settled at Meyersville, DeWitt County, on the north bank of Coleto Creek," Buck once wrote. "Few maps mark Meyersville now, though two or three hundred people still live there. The first Lutheran church there, of which Jacob Schiwetz was a founder, was a log cabin built in 1850—the first Texas church in which the Lutherans worshipped. My grandparents, Wilhelminne and Frederick Philip Schiwetz, are buried in its churchyard."

Buck's father, Berthold Schiwetz, Sr., was a banker in the nearby town of Cuero. His mother, Anne Reiffert Schiwetz, was the daughter of a prosperous German Texas rancher and an accomplished artist in her own right. (You can see her influence in this book, in the delightful little watercolor, *Cabin in the Woods*, page 35, which Buck painted at the age of twelve, under her tutelage.) One of Buck's brothers, Berthold, Jr., before his recent death attained an international reputation as a sculptor of great achievement. His other brothers, while engaged in business, also have earned reputations in creative fields.

Buck holds a degree in architecture from Texas A&M University, where he also completed practically all of the work for an advanced degree in this field. He abandoned the practice of architecture early, to pursue his talent for artistic portrayal of Texas houses and scenes. In the midst of the Great Depression, he took a tilt at the biggest windmill of them all, as a free-lance artist in New York City. Before he was lured back to Texas, he won the praise of nationally recognized critics, sold his work to leading national magazines, and was offered a position on the art faculty of New York University.

He turned his back on New York to return to his beloved homeland and join a couple of old friends in founding a new advertising agency, Franke, Wilkinson & Schiwetz, in booming Houston. The firm grew and prospered, with much credit due to the imaginative and genuinely Texan illustrations from the Schiwetz pen, pencil, and brush. It was the Texas scenes he produced for the advertisements of such clients as Anderson-Clayton, Hughes Tool, Lufkin Foundry, Dow Chemical, Humble, and others, during this period, that endeared him to a wide Texas audience.

Humble, in particular, gave him wide-ranging assignments, throughout the length and breadth of Texas, and capitalized on the individualistic Schiwetz talent for portraying Texas with warmth and wallop. His work was widely published in *The Humble Way* and was preserved in a remarkable company giveaway called *The Texas Sketchbook*. Buck's first hard-bound book of his own work was published in 1960 by the University of Texas Press, under the title *Buck Schiwetz' Texas*. It has gone into several printings and is an acknowledged Texas classic. Later, the same press issued a handsome portfolio of Schiwetz paintings of the Texas missions. The artist also contributed telling illustrations to many books on Texas subjects. You are now holding his second full-length effort as artist-author. It, too, is destined for a lasting audience.

The Houston advertising agency was sold in 1954 to a national concern, McCann Erickson. Buck stayed on for a time, first as art director, then as consultant. When he finally retired, he was offered a position on the art faculty at the University of Houston. He again dodged the academic world and headed for the Hill Country to devote full time to his art.

For quite a few years now, he has been "doing his own thing." Living at Hunt, though they maintain a home in Houston, Buck and Ruby Lee spend much time roaming the state. Buck shoots and collects thousands of pictures and slides and makes delightfully hasty and squiggly little field sketches, carefully annotated, as the basis for future work. Sometimes he stops to make a full-blown pen or pencil sketch, or even a watercolor or a mixed-media painting on the spot. He paints only what he wants to, when he wants to, and is reluctant to sell his works until he has had some time to enjoy them, himself.

Of one such recent trip, Buck wrote: "We followed a usual zig-zag over country farm roads. It's amazing how much they reveal of unheralded scenes." For years, the artist has accumulated his field sketches and photographs, until he has thousands on hand, waiting to be turned into finished paintings when it suits his fancy. Sometimes years, even decades, pass between the making of a field sketch and the final work of art—thirty years, to be exact, in the case of one prized painting. If he ever loses the desire or ability to travel, and still can paint, Schiwetz has the raw material on hand to keep him occupied for another forty years.

The quantity, quality, and diversity of both subject and technique in this man's work are amazing to artists and laymen alike. He has ranged Texas from the High Plains of the Panhandle to the Big Thicket, from the Piney Woods to the Trans-Pecos, and from the Gulf Coast to the Chisos Mountains. He has depicted the desolate ruins of abandoned back-country farmhouses, the honest clean lines of old German homes, the resplendent glories of restored plantations, the dignity and charm of simple country churches, the rococo monstrosities of early court-houses, the charming disarray of small-town Main Streets, and the imposing skylines of teeming cities. You will find all of them in this book, along with recordings of the natural scene, from the wild beauty of the Big Bend to the palm-lined fields of the Rio Grande Valley. The vast treeless sweep of the High Plains stands in contrast to the well-watered glades of deep East Texas. He paints the pelicans at Boca Chica on Padre Island and the roseate spoon-bills at Old Indianola, a profusion of wild flowers in DeWitt County, cattle huddled against the cold in Harris County, and a snowstorm in the sand hills near Sterling City.

All these bright bits and pieces fit together to make the wondrous mosaic that is the Texas scene, as Buck sees it. He sketches cowboys at work in Shackelford County, roughnecks on a drilling rig in the Gulf, and a row-crop farmer plowing the flat vastness near Plainview. In this one volume you will find a representation of an artist's view of our basic industries and agriculture; of our people, the towns and cities they have built, and the countryside that surrounds them.

It is remarkable that Buck never allowed himself to get trapped into a single subject, style, or medium, as many artists do. He has continued to range the stylistic field as widely as he has ranged Texas. His first success, which won national attention, was with his pencil sketches of old and interesting houses. This was an uncrowded field, for which he was especially equipped, because of his training in architecture. He could well have built a successful career on this single accomplishment. But, in this one book you will find Schiwetz watercolors, etchings, oils, lithographs, and mixed-media paintings; there is even one delightful sketch in Crayola, *West Texas* (page 34).

The oldest picture in this collection is a small watercolor, *Cabin in the Woods*, done in DeWitt County in 1910. Its style is the hazy twilight-muted landscape so common to the European artists of a slightly earlier period. It is testimony to the influence of older artists of European background who trained Buck's mother and the china-painting Cuero lady who was his early teacher. During the time in which these ladies took their training, San Antonio boasted such fine artists and teachers as the Dutchman, Robert Onderdonk; the Frenchmen, Theodore Gentilz and Edward Grenet; and the Germans, William C. A. Thielepape, Carl G. von Iwonski, and Herman Lungkwitz. Buck's early pencil sketches are in the mildly romantic vein of European sketches of landmarks and landscapes in that period. Later they became more direct and forceful, though never without a certain aura of charm he could feel, rather than see, in the structure itself.

During his New York sojourn, Buck studied etching and lithography, and he later produced some excellent works like *The Shrimp Fleet Comes In* (page 36), *Gulf Coast Souvenir* (page 46), and *The Bull Wheel* (page 54). Such watercolors as *April in DeWitt County* (frontispiece) and *Coast Guard Station at Matagorda* (page 39) won him international recognition. He combined pastels and ink, as in his *Souvenir of Boca Chica on Padre Island* (page 37), or used ink wash, as in *Waco Suspension Bridge* (page 60). Much of his most recent work, which has a strength and glow distinctively Schiwetzian and definitely different from his earlier work, is in mixed media.

For a time, several years ago, Buck abandoned the representational for a fling at abstract art. This was a tremendous emotional experience for him and resulted in a number of outstanding pieces. "It's like composing music," the artist once wrote. "It is very emotional. But the main thing about abstract art is that so much of it is phony." And later, of his venture into the nonrepresentational, he said, "It contributed an opportunity to release a build-up of surcharged emotions, to find a closer kinship to the abstract, and to engage in color improvisations." One striking abstract, he wrote, "was evolved during what I call my chaotic period, when I felt that I was completely enmeshed with frustrations. It remains my favorite."

The emotional purging of this period seems to have brought to his later work a serenity and a warmth overshadowing his earlier paintings. In many of them, too, you will find an imaginative use of color that is purely emotional. No old tin roof ever had the brilliant rainbow of colors he gave to that in *Fort McKavett Barracks* (page 111), for example. Still, its striking impressionism conveys a genuine feeling from the artist to the viewer.

Over the years, Buck Schiwetz has won and received more honors than come to most men. He has won top prizes in major competitions in many media. He is a member of the distinguished Texas Philosophical Society and has been formally dubbed a Knight of San Jacinto—than which there is no "than whicher" in the lexicon of Texas accolades. He has been acclaimed as "Mr. Texas" by one critic, as the best-known and best-loved artist of his state by many others. He has lived to see his preachments change and humanize the thinking and the way of life of Texans generally. His most recent honor, which had not been formally announced when this was written, was selection by his alma mater for a Distinguished Alumni Award in 1972.

Buck has plowed steadily ahead over the years, despite some very spectacular ups and downs. Like all creative people, he has encountered those frightening plateaus of productivity, which chill the heart with the fear that "the well has gone dry." He has learned to pace himself, to wait out those unproductive times, or to escape the doldrums by switching to a new medium and style. And he has learned to pray very hard. To his amazement, as much as to that of the rest of us, he finds himself, at seventy-four, steady of hand and sharp of eye, capable of producing, at top speed, paintings of striking clarity and force in a style even more alive and exciting than that of his younger years.

"Aleman Titi Grande" has, in truth, burned his candle "at both ends" . . . and often in the middle. "But, . . . oh, my friends— / It gives a lovely light."

R. HENDERSON SHUFFLER
San Antonio, Texas

PLATES

2. West Texas

3. Cabin in the Woods

4. *The Shrimp Fleet Comes In*

5. *Souvenir of Boca Chica on Padre Island*

THE CARETAKERS HOUSE
FT BROWN, BROWNSVILLE

6. *The Caretaker's House, Fort Brown*

7. *Coast Guard Station at Matagorda*

SAN JACINTO MONUMENT AND BATTLESHIP TEXAS.

E.M.Schiwetz 55

8. *San Jacinto Monument and Battleship "Texas"*

9. *Dow Chemical Plant at Freeport*

FISHERMAN SHANTIES
HIGH ISLAND

10. *Fishermen's Shanties, High Island*

11. *Offshore Drilling in the Gulf*

12. *Shrimp and Oyster Fleet, Port O'Connor*

13. *Dry Dock, Aransas Pass*

14. *Gulf Coast Souvenir*

15. *Beach Scene*

SOUVENIR OF GALVESTON

RM Schiwetz '31

16. *Souvenir of Galveston*

17. *Old Flour Bluff*

BACKYARDS & LA FITTE HOUSE - GALVESTON

18. *Backyards and Lafitte House, Galveston*

19. *Summer Pastime*

The Freedom Tree

20. *The Freedom Tree*

21. *Roseate Spoonbills at Old Indianola*

22. *The Bull Wheel*

23. Wet Weather

SAM HOUSTON OAK
GONZALES, TEXAS

24. *Sam Houston Oak, Gonzales*

25. *Sugar Cane Harvest*

26. *Reuben Turner House, Itasca*

27. *East Texas Piney Woods*

28. *Waco Suspension Bridge*

29. *The Mann House at Waco*

30. *Dallas Terminal Station from West Dallas Viaduct*

31. *Towards Talco*

32. Old Hotel and Market, Dallas

33. Souvenir of Yorktown

SHACK OFF JIMTOWN ROAD NEAR DALLAS, TEX

34. *Shack off Jimtown Road near Dallas*

35. *Forgotten*

36. *Von Behr House, Sisterdale*

THE VON BEHR HOUSE
SISTERDALE TEX

37. *The Von Behr House, Sisterdale*

THE DUCHARMES PALM HOUSE — AUSTIN, TE

38. *Ducharmes-Palm House, Austin*

39. *Boulder Outcropping in South Central Texas*

40. *Abner Cook House, Colorado Street, Austin*

41. *Reminiscences of DeWitt County, Texas*

THE OLD FRENCH EMBASSY - AUSTIN

42. *Old French Embassy, Austin*

SOUVENIR OF DOWNTOWN HOUSTON ON DALLAS ST
THE FEDERAL LAND BANK

43. *Downtown Houston on Dallas Street*

44. *President Johnson's Birthplace, Stonewall*

45. *Cotton Gin, Smiley—Vintage of '30*

46. *Study for Main House, LBJ Ranch*

47. *Houston County Courthouse, Crockett*

THE NOBLE HOUSE HOUSTON,

48. *Noble House, Houston*

49. *Old President's Home at A&M*

50. *Liendo*

51. *Lissie*

LA BAHIA - GOLIAD

52. *La Bahía Chapel at Goliad*

53. *Sinclair Refining Company*

Mission La Bahia - Goliad
Before Restoration

54. *Presidio La Bahia before Restoration*

55. *Monsanto Chemical Company*

56. *St. Mary's, Victoria*

57. St. Mary's Church, Victoria

58. DeWitt County Courthouse, Cuero

59. *King Ranch and Oil Operation*

THE OLD DR LAY HOUSE WITH VIEW OF HALLETSVILLE, TEX.

60. *Old Dr. Lay House with View of Hallettsville*

61. *Oil Derricks*

62. *Lambshead Ranch Headquarters*

63. *Lambshead Ranch*

EARLY MORNING AT SPANISH GOURD RANCH

THE REYNOLDS HOUSE WITH WILD TURKEY

64. *Early Morning at Spanish Gourd Ranch, Fort Griffin*

65. *Squaw Tit Mountain*

66. *Bandera County Courthouse*

67. *Winter in Sterling County*

OLD TRINITY UNIVERSITY
AT TEHUACANA

68. Old Trinity University at Tehuacana

69. *Old Dewberry House near Tyler*

THE CAPT. SCHREINER HOME
KERRVILLE TEX

70. *Captain Schreiner Home, Kerrville*

71. *Fredericksburg*

72. *William Pepper Cabin near Marble Falls*

73. *Redbirds on the South Fork*

74. *No. 506 Main Street, Old Log Cabin, Fredericksburg*

75. *Scene on Lone Man Creek*

76. *Aue House, Leon Springs*

For Muriel Reese Bracewell
© Christmas 1967

THE WILSON COUNTY COURTHOUSE – FLORESVILLE

77. *Wilson County Courthouse, Floresville*

78. The Alamo at Night

79. *Fort McKavett Barracks*

E.M.Schiwetz '24

SCENE ON SAN ANTONIO RIVER
SAN ANTONIO TEXAS.

80. Scene on San Antonio River

The Kyser Ruins
Cherry Spring

Buck 69

81. *Kyser Ruins, Cherry Spring*

82. *Many Chimneys, Old San Antonio*

83. *Irish Flat*

84. *A Visit to the Alamo*

85. *Bedding Down*

86. *Mission Concepción*

87. *On the Wareing Place*

88. Scene on San Antonio River

89. *Early Winter on the Guadalupe*

AN FERNANDO CATHEDRAL SAN ANTONIO

FROM COURTHOUSE SQUARE

90. San Fernando Cathedral, San Antonio

91. *Old Barns near Center Point*

92. Excerpts from Fredericksburg Cemetery

93. *Remnants of a Ranch near Fredericksburg*

94. Mission Concepción

TERLINGUA

95. Terlingua

96. *View of Eagle Pass*

The Artist's Comments on His Pictures

NOTES BY THE ARTIST WITH JOHN EDWARD WEEMS

No place that I know of is as colorful as the state of Texas. From the Big Bend of West Texas to the Big Thicket in East Texas, from the Panhandle to the Valley, there is no end to the material upon which to draw.

For more than sixty years—since childhood—I have been sketching and painting the Texas scene. This selection of pictures shows how I have portrayed the state in different media and styles during that time. Some of these pictures I like more than others, but here they all are.

In none of them have I tried to achieve photographic accuracy. Instead, I have concentrated on capturing the spirit of the scene. Sometimes I have moved objects into the picture—buildings, oil derricks, trees—because they intrigued me in some way or because they seemed to belong. In one case (*Souvenir of Yorktown*, page 65) I painted an old fire station from one place, Yorktown, and a backdrop of buildings mostly from another town, Cuero.

People often ask me about this and other phases of my work, and I guess a book covering sixty years of effort would be as good a place as any to reproduce a few personal notes penned several years ago at the request of a writer:

I can attribute whatever fulfillment I have realized in painting to my early ventures in the linear media: namely, pencil etching lithography—basic drawing. This nudged me into further work in architecture and into an absorbing interest in old houses, historic edifices, buildings under con-

struction. Early in my work I made hundreds of these sketches, and I still do today.

The urge to step out into watercolor, to loosen up—to use watercolor for a chaser and a getting-away from the strict regimen of advertising—ushered in a fuller use of color and qualified me as a painter of sorts. The Texas coastal scene was a fertile area, and I put down hundreds of watercolor and pencil pieces. Suddenly I found myself overindulgent in the use of watercolor—even leaning toward virtuosity—and I wanted to break away.

In the mid-1930's I swung into a progression of simulations—Cézanne, Monet, Utrillo, Van Gogh. The works of those artists intrigued me. (Now my favorites are Andrew Wyeth, Edward Hopper, and Norman Rockwell. Rockwell is not in the fine arts realm, maybe, but I like him and own a stack of his reproductions.) I have seldom shown the paintings of my own that I did in the mid-thirties. They did not always strike twelve, and they remain ensconced in my Hunt studio.

Much later I began using the newer painting vehicles—polymer acrylics, felt pencils, oil pastels, and oils with the copal medium. This work calls for patience, but it has been an intriguing experience—a description that could also apply generally to my use of mixed media: first pure watercolor, then opaque color, pastels, inks, and finally the oils.

In the late 1950's I was prevailed upon to move into nonobjective, nonrepresentational work by the Humble Oil Com-

pany people, who wanted a series of panels for the lobby of their new building. About that time I began allocating my working hours to both the objective and the nonobjective, trying to find a compromise—but not a cheap one. Nonrepresentational paintings—abstractions—can be phony, but they delight me when they are honest and in good taste, and when I am able to key in emotionally with them. I have found a new satisfaction in those works.

Still, I have much to learn here. I am a student and shall remain one as long as many approaches dangle before me and new media come into use.

In my years of work I have sketched in many, many places —in New Mexico, New York City and its environs, New England, Mexico, and Europe. But my favorite scenes are in Texas. With this book I hope I might have given Texans a worthy depiction of their great heritage and might have made them more aware of the need for preserving many beautiful old structures that will otherwise fall victim some day soon to the blind bulldozers of progress.

Now for the individual pictures:

April in DeWitt County (frontispiece)

This scene is a compendium of many years' effort in trying to put down in paint a part of Texas. Naturally, DeWitt County (where my birthplace of Cuero is located) would be my favored focal point. When I was a young upstart, an irrepressible youth of ten, we would ride to Grandma's (in Meyersville) in a rented livery-stable surrey, come Easter. The palette of wild flowers was overwhelmingly beautiful along the whole thirteen-mile trek. I made sophomoric watercolors and Crayola studies—but later hid them away.

In this picture (near Lindenau, about two miles off the highway between Cuero and San Antonio) I used the golden-blossomed huisache trees as my lode subject matter. The church was moved about a mile.

West Texas (page 34)

Everybody, it seems, wanted to buy this drawing. They were intrigued by its simplicity. But that was one of the hardest pictures I ever tried to draw—to get that horizon at a comfortable place on the sketch for sound composition and to place that cloud in the right area. I used Crayola.

It was drawn from recollection, after a visit to the Plains Country around Hereford and Plainview. When I made my first trip there, windmills dotted the horizon everywhere. Now there are not so many to be seen. Modern pumps are taking their place.

Cabin in the Woods (page 35)

My mother was a wonderful artist in her own right, but she was thwarted by the demands of family life. I remember that she used to have some beautiful pencil drawings, but she destroyed them. I wish I had them now. I used to study those drawings when I was young.

Her work instigated my enthusiasm for art. *Cabin in the Woods* is one of my early efforts, painted when I was a striving lad of twelve. I remember the scene vividly. I used to see it and others like it on the Meyersville road.

My mother was proud of this and other attempts, but my father showed little interest. He never encouraged me to be an artist. He wanted me to be an engineer—to go into work where it would be possible to have a future, to make some money. Later on, as his son began to gain mention as an artist, he was happy to change his mind. He actually became proud of me—thought I was really something special.

Credit is due to someone else, too. An art instructor at Cuero named Mary Louise Gramann encouraged me after she learned of my interest in drawing. She inspired me to go ahead with this sort of work, and I did half a dozen other pictures like it. She did beautiful china painting—and insisted that I use small, needlepoint brushes for my pictures. I really labored over these things.

After this youthful episode I forgot about art for many, many years—until I went to A&M. I swung instead into the car-designing "business" with two other boys, Tom Stell (who also became an artist) and John Boyd. We were drawing streamlined cars in the days of the Model T, before the word *streamline* had come into use. I have composition books full of those drawings. It was my resolute intention to become a car designer, but later events changed all that.

The Shrimp Fleet Comes In (page 36)

Birds, boats, and water (as you will see in time in these comments) are among my favorite vehicles for adding interest, life, and color to a picture.

This sketch, done in the early 1930's during my etching period, interprets rather than details a Gulf Coast scene.

Souvenir of Boca Chica on Padre Island (page 37)

Frank Fields and I happened upon this tourist mecca while working on the River Road forts assignment for Humble in the early 1950's. We ended our tour with an overnight stay in a Brownsville motel. Scanning the desk post cards there, we noticed a beautiful view of Boca Chica, on Padre Island eighteen miles east of Brownsville—at the very tip of Texas. There was nothing to do but drive over to this tourist heaven the next day.

We were greeted by a sordid array of shacks, myriads of pesky mosquitoes, and many delightful painting subjects. Happily, we were also rewarded with a modicum of drum and catfish. I completed this pastel-and-ink rendition many years after the visit.

The Caretaker's House, Fort Brown (page 38)

Left over from a mostly forgotten past when I sketched it in 1952 was this gaunt, crumbling building at Fort Brown, in Brownsville. It had been built at the site of General Zachary Taylor's "Fort Texas," an earthwork hurriedly thrown up in 1846 on the north bank of the Rio Grande, across the river from the Mexican town of Matamoros (in the background here), to guard against a Mexican attack following Texas annexation. Mexico never had formally recognized the independence of her former territory and was even less likely to approve of its joining the United States.

War did result. During a bombardment of the earthen outpost its temporary commander, Major Jacob Brown, was mortally wounded. The subsequent fort and the town that grew up nearby later carried his name into posterity. Fort Brown also brought fame to William Crawford Gorgas, who was a young first lieutenant and an assistant surgeon when he began his long battle against yellow fever during an epidemic here in the 1880's.

In 1945 the fort became officially and permanently inactivated by the U.S. Army. Its usable buildings eventually were taken over by Texas Southmost College. The only sentinels you will see in the area of old Fort Brown today are tall palm trees like this one—a silent sentinel except when a stiff Gulf breeze rustles the fronds.

Coast Guard Station at Matagorda (page 39)

Vertical projections abound here: the many piles under this old Coast Guard station, which had somehow survived the fury of numerous Gulf storms when I put it down on paper, and the many piles of other structures with less successful pasts. Like the sea birds, buildings along the Texas coast stand on long legs.

This Coast Guard station is the descendant of a U.S. Life Saving Station originally established in 1878.

The surrounding area abounds in history. Alonso Alvarez de Pineda, commissioned by the governor of Jamaica to explore the Gulf Coast, visited Matagorda Island in 1519. René Robert Cavelier, Sieur de La Salle, sailed past the island in 1685 (as many historians say) on his way through Pass Cavallo to Lavaca Bay and the founding of Fort Saint Louis. Long afterward, following Anglo-Saxon settlement of the area, a health resort was established on the island—in the 1850's—but a tropical hurricane blew it away.

San Jacinto Monument and Battleship "Texas" (page 40)

An assignment resulted in this sketch of a scene many tourists have seen, although probably not from this angle.

The shaft (570 feet high) marks the site of Sam Houston's decisive victory over Santa Anna. The ship was added to the scene in 1948 when the State Legislature provided a permanent berth for the U.S.S. Texas, a battleship in commission from 1914 through World War II, when she participated in five invasions.

Dow Chemical Plant at Freeport (page 41)

During my copious work for Dow Chemical I painted this scene of their Freeport plant as viewed from the high bridge leading to Surfside over the Intracoastal Canal (now more properly called the Gulf Intracoastal Waterway).

I always have liked this picture as one of my better interpretations of the Texas industrial scene. I wanted to convey the soggy sky—not paint an exquisite blue Texas sky clouded with distant thunderheads—and I think it came off well here. I was trying to show the heat and humidity of the Gulf

Coast, where you often see ocher-colored skies and skies that are almost brown—not poetic blue.

At their Freeport plant the Dow people convert sea water, oyster shell, and natural gas into magnesium metal, plastics, fertilizer, antifreeze, and many other intermediate and finished products.

Fishermen's Shanties, High Island (page 42)

Across the bay from Galveston, High Island provided an abundance of colorful sketching material in the 1930's before a series of hurricanes blew the scenery away. The flimsy shacks with their improvisations, the rusted weather vanes, rickety vehicles, abandoned boats, bait boxes adorned with shells—all attracted me.

The island earned its name by being the highest point (forty-seven feet) between Point Bolivar and Sabine Pass. Years ago residents of Bolivar Peninsula would gather there for shelter during Gulf storms, but their refuge never was a very safe one.

Offshore Drilling in the Gulf (page 43)

For hours I flew around in one of those little Bell helicopters observing this scene and taking color pictures for future reference. I snapped many, many shots from all directions. This view actually appealed to me less than some of the others, but here it is.

I painted this loose watercolor from the snapshots. Because of the highly technical nature of the subject it was a "booger" to do. Fortunately, there were many sea birds fluttering around. I always utilize them whenever I can.

Shrimp and Oyster Fleet, Port O'Connor (page 44)

Rummaging around the Gulf Coast country resulted in this ink-wash drawing. I just happened to be poking about

the fish houses at Port O'Connor when I stumbled onto this scene—or at least one very much like it. I moved the boats around a bit in my picture to get better composition.

Some time after I sketched this the houses and boats were obliterated by one of those deadly hurricanes. The area has been rebuilt, but it does not offer the same scene.

Dry Dock, Aransas Pass (page 45)

Boats always have intrigued me, whatever their designation—tug, shrimp, oyster—and whether in dry dock or awash. They provide colorful sketching material.

This Aransas Pass scene was captured before Hurricane Celia thrashed the Corpus Christi area. I have no idea what it might look like now. The cross-topped shaft in the background stands as a memorial to fishermen who died in their arduous work.

Gulf Coast Souvenir (page 46)

Ruby Lee and I drove to Port Lavaca in the late 1920's and I was fascinated as usual by the coastal scene: the fish house (as I called it) and windmill, the two men and those oyster shells, the boats, and the nets (hung up to dry) waving in the breeze.

The derricks actually did not exist at this location. I saw them farther away on the coastal prairie, in the Placedo oil field (Victoria County), but I thought I would bring them in here. They seemed emblematic of the coastal scene at that time, and I wanted to depict an area—not just a few thousand square feet of Port Lavaca.

Beach Scene (page 47)

Before being built up with shanties West Beach in Galveston was as clean as a whistle. You could drive down it for miles and miles and see nothing but the light gray-green water of the Gulf off to your left, maybe a few puffs of clouds in the sky, and white sand dunes like these, sprinkled with only sparse vegetation. The brightness of the scene would put a squint in your eyes.

Occasionally you might happen upon fishermen seining in the shallow surf. What a sight it was to see them pulling in those nets loaded with thrashing fish! This watercolor, painted in 1931, is a memento of long-past days spent on a magnificent beach.

Souvenir of Galveston (page 48)

You will not see the old, abandoned wagons in Galveston today, but some shuttered shacks are still there (as they are all along the Gulf Coast)—although maybe not these. I did this pencil sketch in 1931.

Timeworn buildings make good subject material. They have character. There has been—and still is—more life in those old shanties than in smooth, faceless modern construction.

Old Flour Bluff (page 49)

Years ago you could have driven six or seven miles southeast of Corpus Christi—down Ocean Drive along the bay—and viewed this scene at Old Flour Bluff. I drove down there often and fished in the shallows for speckled trout.

I also liked to portray the locale in watercolor. The fish houses made wonderful subjects; the broken, overturned boats intrigued me (they are always good vehicles for painting, if not for transportation); and the colors are magnificent. I did have many more watercolors of Old Flour Bluff —and I thought they were beautiful—but they have disappeared.

Like my paintings, Old Flour Bluff itself has vanished. This scene can no longer be viewed except in this watercolor.

Backyards and Lafitte House, Galveston (page 50)

Clutter makes good subject matter for me: old fences, barrels, tubs—general disarray. I don't like anything slick.

Probably only the name and the location at 1415 Avenue A in Galveston associated this Lafitte House with the Gulf pirates Jean and Pierre Lafitte. Jean Lafitte (or Laffite) did establish a privateering base on Galveston Island before 1820, prior to the founding of the city, and he built an expansive Maison Rouge (Red House) as his headquarters. The last vestiges disappeared many years ago—swept clean by hurricanes. An early map of Galveston prepared by W. H. Sandusky showed the site of Maison Rouge to have been between Fourteenth and Fifteenth streets on Avenue A. This house, which I sketched years ago, was built on the supposed site.

Francis Sheridan, an English visitor to Galveston twenty years after Jean Lafitte lived there, saw what he identified as the scant remains of Lafitte's base and the nearby wreck of a vessel built entirely of mahogany. "All traces . . . will soon be gone," Sheridan wrote in his journal, and he was right.

Summer Pastime (page 51)

For five or six years around the time I painted this scene (1931) I worked in pure watercolor and used a great deal of white space on my paper. (These productions are called aquarelles.) It was an era I went through.

I became so engrossed with pure watercolor that I told myself one day, "You're trying to be a virtuoso with the darn stuff." I quit it. Thus I escaped the fate of some other artists I have observed. They were too immaculate—and afraid of mixed media. I preferred to get to something heavier.

The Freedom Tree (page 52)

Under the umbrella thrown up by this moss-covered oak tree still standing near the Brazos River, slaves of a Fort Bend County plantation heard the words that gave them their freedom. This picture appeared earlier in a book, *The Freedom Tree*, by Edward Hutcheson of Houston.

The region abounds in history. The present site of Richmond, county seat of Fort Bend, is in the area of the original settlement of Stephen F. Austin's "Old Three Hundred"— holders of land grants in his first colony.

Roseate Spoonbills at Old Indianola (page 53)

Well into the fall of one year I spotted these roseate spoonbills mingling with flocks of other birds. It was an unusual sight, because the spoonbills are known to leave the coast in July—or at least by August—for other areas much farther south.

I have painted roseate spoonbills often, but they are rarities. When you do see them you usually see thirty or forty together. Their colors are splendid—deep pink wings, burnt orange tails, pale yellow heads and bills.

The Bull Wheel (page 54)

This might be one of the few remaining bull wheels (if it is still there)—an intriguing relic of early oil production. I found it at historic Spindletop, an old field ripe with remnants left over from an earlier day: wooden derricks, tanks, antiquated machinery—all in seeming repose in an area permeated by the smell of low-gravity oil.

Spindletop, near Beaumont, has calmed down. But on January 10, 1901, it was a bedlam. A well being drilled by A. F. Lucas erupted with a deafening roar, hurling a mixture of oil, gas, mud, and rocks hundreds of feet into the air. For six days the gusher remained uncapped; more than 75,000 barrels of oil flowed freely each day, forming a deep, black, squishy lake around the well. Spindletop land sold for anywhere from $200,000 to $900,000 an acre. Modern oil production had come into being, but today silence encompasses Spindletop.

Probably not even this old bull wheel has been thoroughly appreciated by the people who have seen it. When I visited the place someone told me that there used to be two of these relics, but one very cold night a nightwatchman chopped up the other wheel and built himself a fire with it.

I took some liberties myself with the old thing. In this picture I moved it for the sake of getting a good background.

Wet Weather (page 55)

This is purely an improvisation. It represents no particular locale. Instead, it interprets a scene (in this case a bay front) by putting in all the needed ingredients. The house came from one place, the windmill from another, the boat from still another—and so on.

Sam Houston Oak, Gonzales (page 56)

Around Peach Creek east of Gonzales—off U.S. Highway 90A—stands a majestic oak tree near which Sam Houston and his men rested during the early morning hours of March 14, 1836, at the beginning of their long retreat (from Santa Anna's invading army) that ended in the Battle of San Jacinto more than a month later.

I like this drawing of the old tree. The style is free and easy—and the oak itself is wonderful.

Sugar Cane Harvest (page 57)

This scene is typical of the sugar cane harvest that occurs in deep southeast Texas and bordering areas of Louisiana. I think this scene might actually be in Louisiana, but it doesn't make any difference and I am happy someone decided to include it in the book. (Maybe a $150 frame provided adequate persuasion, but my viewers and readers will be unable to draw similar benefit from it.) I like it as a picture—like it for its color and for the type of painting it is.

Reuben Turner House, Itasca (page 58)

Typical of homes built in eastern areas of Texas more than a century ago is this magnificent old house about five miles from Itasca, in Hill County. Probably it was a home wonderful to live in, with a long gallery (or porch) in front for relaxing in summer breezes and fireplaces inside for winter warmth. Its beautiful scale still shows through. That and the timber and the rock work in the chimneys originally attracted me.

The grave of Mr. Stubblefield, an early settler, actually lay about five hundred yards from the house. I moved it in closer, to get it in the picture.

When I last saw this old home it had been abandoned for many years and was being used as a hay barn.

East Texas Piney Woods (page 59)

My brother-in-law, Robert "Slats" Sanders, accompanied me on my first forays deep into East Texas, in 1929—or maybe I should say I accompanied him, because he had the car: a Star roadster. It looked fragile, but it got us over unimproved East Texas roads that in wet weather could turn gooey.

Since then I have come to know the area well. I am fascinated by its history and by some examples of early architecture like the Epperson House and the Presbyterian Church in Jefferson, the Barry House in Marshall, the Cartwright House in San Augustine, and others. But the countryside itself offers excellent material, too, for sketches and paintings, particularly with the use of color. The green backdrop formed by pine trees casts pastel reflections in the quiet pools and lakes that abound in the area and makes the clean white of the dogwood blossoms more striking in contrast. Cranes, herons, and smaller colorful birds decorate the scene.

In this painting I sought to depict East Texas as it is today: an old, early-settled region still largely covered with forests, but one now bustling with industry and commerce centering on petroleum, lumbering, and wood products.

Waco Suspension Bridge (page 60)

When Waco denizens got together money for spanning the Brazos River in 1870, they could boast of having what was known at that time as the world's longest suspension bridge. It was considered a great engineering accomplishment and won the title of "magic bridge." Waco commerce boomed; people came many miles out of their way to take advantage of such an easy crossing of so tricky a river.

The steel cables came from New York, but the bricks for anchor towers were made in Waco. The same builders also constructed the Brooklyn Bridge.

As I write this the bridge is still in use.

The Mann House at Waco (page 61)

Texas-style galleries and the magnificent trees impressed me immediately. The John Wesley Mann House (also known as East Terrace) was built in Waco on Mill Street overlooking the Brazos River in 1867. Levee and belvedere were constructed along with it. The pleasing pink brick was made on the grounds.

The interior is handsome: graceful stairway, double parlor with ballroom, built-in bath decorated with cherubs.

The architecture shows a reaction against the square, boxlike appearance of some early homes. You can also notice vertical projections—long, narrow windows and doors.

On my first visit I could not sketch the house. Leaves gave the trees a full green coat, and I could not get a view of the place. Later I went back (in 1962, as guest of the Waco Heritage Society) and got this picture.

Dallas Terminal Station from West Dallas Viaduct (page 62)

In the 1920's I was a fledgling draftsman with Thomson and Swaine, architects. I must have encountered a paucity of subject matter to move onto this scene—an early, meticulous pencil drawing of the Dallas Union Station.

But I have always been fascinated by trains. When I was a student at Texas A&M I used freight trains for holiday trips from College Station to Cuero and back—and on weekends rode freights from College Station to Dallas or Houston or wherever they were going, just to get away. I have covered much of the state by train—boxcar, Pullman coach, and cowcatcher.

One of the most depressing developments of this century has been the appearance of diesel engines, with all their blatant sounds. I liked to hear those old steam-locomotive whistles and the happy ringing of bells.

Towards Talco (page 63)

This scene I painted for Standard Oil years ago, deleting from it some extraneous things like an obtrusive truck that stood in the way.

Also absent are oil derricks, but they actually can be found in the vicinity here. Talco, near the Sulphur River in the northeastern part of Texas, was the scene of a major oil discovery in 1936.

Old Hotel and Market, Dallas (page 64)

You could look a long time in Dallas today for a scene like this and still not find it.

In the 1920's I was getting my professional career underway in that city. I was not inundated with work and had plenty of time to wander around in search of subjects to sketch. I was looking for interesting material, not necessarily historical buildings, and chanced upon this scene on Royal Street—known then especially for its many colorful markets.

Souvenir of Yorktown (page 65)

Demolishing this beautiful old Yorktown fire station was almost an act of sheer vandalism, but it happened. I wish I could have been there to salvage it. As far as I know, this

picture and some others I have painted and sketched are the only reminders of a building that should have been allowed to stand.

Yorktown had the fine fire station, but no backdrop. I brought in buildings from Cuero, mostly from the back end of town, and painted this scene, using palette knife on paper —another era I went through, around the mid-1940's.

Shack off Jimtown Road near Dallas (page 66)

In 1926 I spotted this interesting old home from a distance, went by for a closer look, and sketched it. The house shows the architecture of early-day Texas—long front gallery, good use of timber, chimneys at both sides of a rectangular house. That wonderful oak enhanced the scene. At this time I was deep in the throes of pencil work.

I tried to find out something about the history of the house, but nobody was at home. I have not been back since.

Forgotten (page 67)

This is a barn behind an old house near Hunt. Once I took a sketching class out there, and I did this particular picture.

In something like this I use many improvisations, inserting chickens, goats, tractors, old trailers, and the like. I have a tremendous file of these subjects collected during years of work. Not so long ago I was looking through my pictures and found a sketch of an old steam tractor.

Von Behr House, Sisterdale (page 68)

A good part of old Sisterdale, in Kendall County, remains.

Nicolas Zink established the community in 1847. He built several log cabins in the vicinity. The last time I was there, one of Zink's cabins still stood, but shakily.

In the two or three years following his founding of Sisterdale a number of well-educated Germans settled in the area. John R. Bartlett, appointed commissioner by President Zachary Taylor to run the boundary between the United States and Mexico, visited the community in 1850 and later wrote about it as a center of learning and culture. So did Frederick Olmsted, who visited Sisterdale in the mid-1850's.

I had examined the place a number of times, but not until Mrs. Max Poss and Sam Woolford of Boerne showed me around and told me something of the history did I really get to know much about it. I was delighted with their stories and with the scenery.

The Von Behr House, which I have used as pictured here on a Christmas card, proved impressive. Another version of this same house appears on page 69.

The Von Behr House, Sisterdale (page 69)

This house is emblematic of the solidity and the thoughtful design characterized by the early architecture of this area. I like the barn, too.

This is one of my favorite pictures. Actually I hate to sell drawings I like—hate to part with them. I often think I am not going to sell any more until my meal gets so low in the barrel that I have to.

Ducharmes-Palm House, Austin (page 70)

When I sketched extensively in Austin in 1951 this house ranked alongside the French Embassy (one of the oldest houses still standing there), the Pease Mansion (designed by that advocate of the Greek Revival, Abner Cook, who also planned other Austin homes), the Swisher House, and other structures as one of the most interesting old homes in the city. It was built (at 206 East Ninth Street) by a Frenchman named Ducharmes, whose devout Catholic wife insisted that the residence be constructed as near as possible to a church.

Walls were built of stone and covered with stucco. Doors, windows, and hardware were brought from France.

Albert Sidney Johnston once lived in the house. Later it was sold to a relative of Svante Palm, the noted book collector of early Austin.

Boulder Outcropping in South Central Texas (page 71)

I never would have stumbled onto this scene except for Virginia Allen, who directed me to it—in a remote location on a ranch in the Llano area. Whether there is any great significance to the rock I am unable to say, but it certainly is different. The color is indigo, garnished with patches and veins of a rusty hue. To me the boulder looked more like a giant piece of lava rock than anything else.

The water (which really was there) gave extra dimension to the picture. Without it there would not have been much to work with—just that rock and the tree.

I love water anyway. I like to work reflections into it.

Abner Cook House, Colorado Street, Austin (page 72)

Abner Cook was the Austin builder who left behind in the city some fine examples of Greek Revival architecture, characterized by those many magnificent Ionic and Doric columns. One of his best-known buildings is the Governor's Mansion at Eleventh and Colorado streets, erected in 1853 on a grand scale that is evident today.

Cook's own home on Colorado Street (near the Mansion) was less impressive, but it still showed his touch when I sketched it years ago. Lumber for the house, which was built originally for another owner, was sawed by hand at Bastrop and transported to Austin.

Reminiscences of DeWitt County, Texas (page 73)

The subject matter came from different places—some from memories covering much more than half a century,

some from earlier pictures in my files. This is another of my improvisations—an interpretation of a scene, not a photographic representation of it.

People often ask how I produce my pictures. I do field work for all of them. Preliminary sketches help, of course. When I have time I often complete a picture right on the job. I avoid drawing very early or very late in the day. (And I don't care for sunrises or sunsets. They can be handled better with photography.)

Usually, I take quite a few snapshots to imbue myself with the scene. It becomes a part of me—I don't unsnap it and go back later.

I teach that method in my classes: take photographs right and left, but don't follow them literally. I am a strong advocate of having photographs available—but departing from them for purposes of interpretation.

Old French Embassy, Austin (page 74)

At San Marcos and East Eighth streets in Austin still stands one of the first houses built in the capital city—the Old French Embassy, erected in 1841 for occupancy by Alphonse de Saligny, chargé d'affaires to the Texas Republic.

You can still see France in the building: double doors opening onto the gallery and French windows in the dormers. Pine lumber went into the central construction, rock into the foundation and the chimneys. Doors, windows, and hardware came straight from France.

The lattice work is no longer there, but it should have been left intact. Its absence robs the house of essential character.

Downtown Houston on Dallas Street (page 75)

For eighteen years after I painted this remarkable old house (in 1953) it was allowed to stand and serve as a cafeteria next-door to the Federal Land Bank in Houston—the building to the right. But after all that time the house

was removed from the scene, although efforts were made by some individuals to save it.

This is typical of the treatment given to so many fine old structures in our state. Some day more Texans will awaken to the beauties of protecting the worthier vestiges of their wonderful heritage, but it might be too late to matter much.

President Johnson's Birthplace, Stonewall (page 76)

The thirty-sixth president of the United States was born in the room to the right on August 27, 1908.

His birthplace, thoroughly restored, is another Gillespie County attraction, open to the public.

Cotton Gin, Smiley—Vintage of '30 (page 77)

A cotton gin with water tank, boilers, and stacks is nothing more than an interesting old relic. Almost everything is electric in a gin these days.

Many, many years ago in Roswell I worked in a gin run by steam. I used to fire up the engine, and it was a beautiful sight to see that old piston working furiously—like one on a side-wheel steamer.

The gin pictured here was one I came across at Smiley, in Gonzales County. The cotton bale really had been left there. It seemed strange that nobody had picked it up, but I have seen as many as a dozen forgotten bales lying around like this.

I loved those old cotton gins, but like many other historical delights they are gone now.

Study for Main House, LBJ Ranch (page 78)

All was bustle in this area when I sketched the Lyndon Johnsons' ranch home in 1964. Mr. Johnson had just become president; extensive communications facilities had been installed here; Secret Service agents were all over the place. But I was given quiet sketching, and this picture indicates nothing of the tremendous activity. Sometimes in those days it seemed that this house was the capital of the world.

The ranch is still closed to the public, of course, but the house can be glimpsed from a distance—from a public road that also runs by President Johnson's birthplace, pictured on page 76.

Houston County Courthouse, Crockett (page 79)

Of all the courthouses I have depicted I believe this was the first one. I saw it initially in the mid-1920's, before the bricks had been painted. Two years later I looked at it again and saw that someone had decided to give it this coat of lemon color. Actually, it did not seem bad.

I decided to paint this particular edifice because it looked like an easy one to do. Unlike most courthouses it was not very ornate. One Sunday morning I noticed those two men on the steps and went to work.

I could never paint with these pure oils again. This was another one of my eras, like the pure-watercolor stage.

Lately, I have returned to Crockett and have observed that this old courthouse no longer stands. It seems that more people of Houston County should have an affection for the old: their county was originally established during the days of the Republic of Texas, in 1837.

Noble House, Houston (page 80)

The first time I saw the Noble House in Sam Houston Park in the late 1920's it had deteriorated badly. Built of brick in 1847, it should have been in a better state—should have had better care.

In the 1930's and 1940's some attempts—mostly inadequate—were made to preserve the house. Not until 1950 did it get the care it deserved, when the Harris County Heritage and Conservation Society made a careful restoration. My only regret about this is that someone did not leave unpainted at least a segment of the raw-brick exterior. The

handmade brick had color and warmth that should have been commemorated somehow.

Old President's Home at A&M (page 81)

In 1963 fire badly damaged this old house, and I had to make my sketch a reconstruction, using old photographs. It took me about five years altogether to finish this—a difficult drawing.

The first occupant was General Lawrence Sullivan "Sul" Ross, who became president of A&M in 1891 after a life full of fighting Comanches, serving as a Texas Ranger, participating in Civil War battles (for the South), and fulfilling the duties of McLennan County sheriff, state senator, and Texas governor.

During my time at A&M (beginning in 1917) the residence was occupied by Dr. and Mrs. W. B. Bizzell. I enjoyed a few visits there, trying to round out a curriculum. My father had sent me to college with the practical goal of making an electrical engineer out of me—no artist for him. But the results quickly proved so disastrous that Dr. Bizzell counseled Papa into letting me change to architecture, an event that saved my collegiate life and eventually allowed me to go into art anyway.

Last residents of the house were the late President and Mrs. Earl Rudder, who occupied it at the time of the fire.

Liendo (page 82)

When I first visited this historic home near Hempstead in the mid-1930's it was a shambles—practically written off. But Liendo was (and is) one of the finest examples of Texas antebellum plantation architecture.

The name came from José Justo Liendo, the first owner (in 1830) of the land on which the house stands. But Leonard W. Groce built the residence—with slave labor—in 1853. In its construction he used Georgia long-leaf pine and bricks made from red clay of the nearby Brazos River.

Bricks stuccoed with red plaster went into the foundation; bricks plastered with lime formed the chimneys. Groce had the inside walls smoothly coated with more plaster, and on the drawing-room ceiling he put an ornate decoration of roses and morning-glories, hand-painted.

Liendo has had a long line of owners, but the most famous were Elisabet Ney, the sculptress, and her husband, Dr. Edmund Montgomery. They bought the house and eleven hundred acres of land from Leonard W. Groce, Jr., for $10,000 in 1874—four years after they had fled to the United States from Germany because of Miss Ney's political troubles. At Liendo Dr. Montgomery not only farmed (as well as he was able) but also conducted scientific research and wrote scientific and philosophical pieces until his death in 1911.

Elisabet Ney could not produce her sculpture in such sterile isolation. For nineteen years she neglected it, devoting herself with more failure than success to raising her children. In the 1890's she moved to Austin, established a studio, and returned to her work, visiting Liendo and her husband occasionally. But when she died in 1907 she was buried at Liendo in a grove of live oaks—as was Dr. Montgomery four years later.

When I made this sketch Liendo belonged to the Carl Deterings of Houston. They have given the old home a thorough and thoughtful going over, so that it can take its rightful place in our Texas architectural heritage.

Lissie (page 83)

In the middle of the rice fields between Eagle Lake and East Bernard on U.S. Highway 90A stood this processor—in the community of Lissie. What caught my attention was the coloring in the corrugated tin. But much of this picture is improvised. I enhanced my color, as I always do with a bleak scene like this. Abstract approach enables me to bring it off.

The bird life of that particular area also fascinated me. It always has. The air was filled with swirling, valooping rice-birds and cowbirds. I utilize them often (as you probably have noticed) as vehicles of character and movement, and to kill a dead area—blank sky.

Lissie seems an odd name for a community, but there is a reason for it. Originally named New Philadelphia when settled in 1875, it was renamed Lissie in 1890 in honor of the first schoolteacher, whose formal name was Malissa C. Leveridge.

La Bahía Chapel at Goliad (page 84)

My father was fascinated by La Bahía, beautifully situated on a high point above the San Antonio River a few miles from Goliad. When I lived in Cuero we often drove there on Sunday afternoons, negotiating the thirty miles in our ponderous 1914 Cadillac in two and a half hours.

The caretaker at La Bahía then was an old man named Tobey Pérez. He was a walking encyclopedia of information (not all of it pure fact) about the place. One of my father's particular delights was listening to the old man talk about La Bahía—and Papa sought to instill the love of that history into me.

He must have succeeded. La Bahía is one of my favorite historical sites. But the best-known story associated with the place is not a pleasant one. After James Fannin and more than three hundred men surrendered in an 1836 battle with a large Mexican army, the Texans were held prisoners in Presidio La Bahía—many of them in this chapel—for one week. Then, on Palm Sunday, March 27, 1836, most of them were marched out and shot by order of Santa Anna.

When I first saw La Bahía the scene was one of desolation almost equal to the history. The chapel stood, but the presidio walls lay in crumbled ruin. Since that time I have made many drawings of the place, but I have never been really happy with any of them. La Bahía just overwhelms me.

Another view of it appears on page 86.

Sinclair Refining Company (page 85)

This is representative of the Houston industrial scene—catalytic fractionating units at Pasadena. In the giant "cat crackers," boilers, heaters, and stills, crude oil is converted into gasolines, lubricating and fuel oils, greases, and waxes.

I have covered industry pretty well, mostly on assignment. The companies have used these pictures in their annual reports and other publications. This drawing is similar to the one on page 87, including the media used: pencil and watercolor.

Industrial scenes are hard to do—they are so highly technical. Before I begin the sketching I roam around, looking for good pictorial aspect. The main considerations in this work are deletion (indicating details rather than relying on meticulous mechanical or engineering drawing) and conveying the idea of activity.

Presidio La Bahía before Restoration (page 86)

After some earlier attempts to refurbish Presidio La Bahía, the entire area has been magnificently and expensively restored. It is open to the public as a national historical landmark.

Appreciation for the restoration is due to numerous individuals. The Most Reverend Mariano S. Garriga, bishop of Corpus Christi and the first native Texan bishop, originally urged the work. Mrs. Kathryn Stoner O'Connor of Victoria financed the four-year project with a $1 million gift; and her nephew, Kemper Williams of Victoria, helped in the undertaking. Architect Raiford Stripling of San Augustine, an authority on restorations, supervised the rebuilding. He and his men dug out the three-acre plot to a depth of eight feet, working carefully all the time, and uncovered five thousand artifacts—most of them on exhibit today in the La Bahía museum. Stripling and his men (most of them Mexican Americans from the Goliad area) used an old map of the place for the rebuilding, and the result has been an accurate restoration displaying some of the most beautiful rock work I have ever seen.

A larger view of the chapel appears on page 84.

Monsanto Chemical Company (page 87)

The commentary just given for Sinclair Refining Company (page 85) could apply here, too.

In industrial scenes I usually look for additional color—something like lagoons with pelicans. (Dow Chemical Plant at Freeport—page 41—might show you what I mean.) But it is not always possible to inculcate this material.

St. Mary's, Victoria (page 88)

The town of Victoria, thirty miles from Cuero, was the destination of some of my very earliest safaris. I remember as a teen-ager being allowed to drive a group of seven persons from Cuero to Victoria for a matinee showing of The Birth of a Nation one weekend. It was a memorable movie, an unforgettable experience, and a time of great responsibility on my part—nothing to be taken lightly.

During those early treks to Victoria I saw St. Mary's Church many times. Even then I was always impressed by the scene. Many years later I did this ink wash from an architectural standpoint, to capture the scope—the magnitude—of the church. You might want to compare it with the watercolor on page 89. Both pictures were done the same year, 1962.

St. Mary's Church, Victoria (page 89)

One wet morning I saw St. Mary's Church with these Mexican Americans bedding down where they had stopped their trucks. I just stared, spellbound by the scene. This very loose watercolor was the result—a wet and an ethnic approach. I wanted to get more of a mood in this picture than in the architectural sketch on the preceding page.

Victoria's religious heritage is mostly Catholic. A large part of the early population was Mexican, Irish, and Italian. St. Mary's Church was originally established in 1824.

The town also was founded that same year, by the *empresario* Martín de León, at a luxuriant site on the Guadalupe River. The settlement was named for Guadalupe Victoria, a president of Mexico, and it remained "Victoria" even during and after the heat of the Texas Revolution.

DeWitt County Courthouse, Cuero (page 90)

From my earliest remembrance I have been impressed by the stately old courthouse in my hometown of Cuero—even before historical edifices meant anything to me. The impressive clock tower gave the old building an appropriate look of presiding over a domain, and a bell there tolled the hours with a wonderful tone that defied all competition. Trees and a lush valley setting enhanced the grandeur.

If history seems to permeate the scene, it does. Historians think that Cabeza de Vaca penetrated DeWitt County in 1528. The first white settlers came in 1825, when the cannibalistic Karankawa Indians were a threat. German immigration began during the days of the Republic of Texas, and today most residents are of that extraction.

DeWitt County itself dates from 1846, when it was formally organized. Cuero became the county seat in 1876, twenty-two years before my own irrepressible arrival on the scene.

King Ranch and Oil Operation (page 91)

The million-acre-plus King Ranch that sprawls over four South Texas counties means more than just cattle. Hundreds of wells produce oil on its lands, and the ranch has become a preserve for wild turkeys, deer, antelope, duck, and other wildlife.

During my visit to the ranch in the late 1950's with Frank Fields, in search of material for an issue of *The Humble Way*, I got lost. I never saw so many gates to go through—fifty or sixty, as I remember, with an array of keys to try at each locked gate.

Old Dr. Lay House with View of Hallettsville (page 92)

Two objects in this scene caught my eye—the distant courthouse tower and the old home that is more properly referred to as the Lay-Bozka House, on U.S. Highway 90A. I have used this drawing on a Christmas card.

Because of the view, I like to enter Hallettsville from the south—from either Victoria or Yoakum. You pass this intriguing Victorian house with its mansard roof, built for Dr. James Lay in 1878, then turn left and go into town by the back way. Ahead looms the impressive Lavaca County courthouse tower.

Oil Derricks (page 93)

Another one of my eras is the impressionistic. People seem to like these paintings.

They are entirely emotional—and I am interested in the emotional experience. This painting is my favorite of the lot. It is not nonrepresentational at all, but I think it is all right. I got "cute" with it—gave it a flare, trying to be sensational.

Impressionistic paintings are fun to do. I just have to have a change occasionally from the literal. Sometimes I get up in the morning and want to do something like this—then have to spend maybe a week at it, thinking about it and improvising the color. Probably, Indians produced their colorful blankets from the same sort of thought.

For this picture I had no particular locale in mind. It is simply a matter of construction and color improvisation. That watery look in the foreground might make *Oil Derricks* more symbolic of the California coast—maybe around Long Beach—than of Texas.

Lambshead Ranch Headquarters (page 94)

I have visited this notable ranch near Albany several times during my safaris into the region of the Clear Fork of the Brazos in search of the magnificent frontier architecture still to be found there, both in ruins and in excellent restorations. My first visit came some years ago at the invitation of Watt Matthews (of Lambshead Ranch) when he, Carl Hertzog, and I collaborated on a revised edition of *Interwoven*, Sallie Reynolds Matthews' narrative of pioneer life. Later I went back on assignment for *The Humble Way* and sketched this view of the headquarters building and other ranch scenes.

People live comfortably and contemporarily on the ranch now, as this drawing and the watercolor on the next page might indicate. They use modern equipment like pasture telephones, trucks, and other machines in their work, as well as horses. But there has been another day here. A hundred or more years ago this establishment was known as the Old Stone Ranch—and no Anglo settlements of note existed between it and Santa Fe, some five hundred miles away in New Mexico. Indians posed a constant threat to Old Stone Ranch inhabitants, who had only the meager protection of a chain of frontier outposts like nearby Fort Griffin.

When I last visited, the ruins of Old Stone Ranch headquarters could still be seen in a pasture near Walnut Creek.

Lambshead Ranch (page 95)

Watt Matthews wanted an overall picture of his ranch. The only way we could get it was to go up in John Brittingham's Piper Cub for an aerial view. Round and round and round we flew—for that article in *The Humble Way*.

My visit aground was a much more delightful experience.

The Shackelford County area afforded me a fine opportunity to study some of the better items of indigenous Texas architecture. Watt Matthews (who is a joy to be around) merits a vote of thanks for keeping as much of the scene intact as he possibly could.

Early Morning at Spanish Gourd Ranch near Fort Griffin (page 96)

While sketching around Shackelford County for *Interwoven*, I stayed upstairs in the attic—the official hostelry—of this old house, a relic from the early Reynolds-Matthews ranching operations.

It is an exquisite, fascinating little place: kitchen with utensils still hanging near the fireplace ready for use, beautiful stairway, dormer windows in the attic. The compactness and simplicity intrigued me.

Over a fireplace in the living room (I believe it was) stood a little doll, attractively dressed, given those early settlers by the Indians, who made it. The doll looked mummified.

Early inhabitants of this area made friends with Indians, but they had their tribulations with them, too. Fort Griffin nearby (originally named Camp Wilson, in 1867) was established to give protection. In its heyday its facilities included barracks for half a dozen companies of cavalry and a band, officers' quarters, hospital, storehouses, guardhouse, pens for animals, magazines, living quarters for laundresses, and other buildings. In the early 1880's Fort Griffin was abandoned, after the Indian threat had waned, but its remains can still be seen.

Squaw Tit Mountain (page 97)

West of Ozona in the arid oil-field area of Iraan-Bakersfield stands this mountain. I became so fascinated by the scene—the old cable rig and all—that I could not get away from it.

Actually I moved in the refinery and the shacks to bring more color, more life. All that, along with the high color evident in the painting, was meant to convey atmosphere—and not to provide a photographic duplication of a scene.

Bandera County Courthouse (page 98)

My drawing of this courthouse is the result of a trip Ruby Lee and I made some years ago to her old home. She spent part of her childhood in Bandera.

While we were parked in front of the house where she once lived, studying it, I happened to catch this view of the courthouse with the tree and the trucks and the trailers. I said to her then it would make a good subject. I had passed the building many times before and never intended to sketch it, but I never had seen it this way.

Ruby Lee used to swing in the oak tree when she was a child. The tree is a little fuller now than it was when I first drew it.

I learned much of the history of the town and the county of Bandera years ago from Marvin Hunter. The first settlers in the vicinity were shinglemakers, who set up a camp amid the verdancy of the Medina River valley in 1852. Two years later a colony of Mormons settled at Bandera. In 1855 sixteen Polish families came to work in the sawmill and established a community of their own. A reminder of those Polish days in Bandera is the fine old Jureczki House.

The fascinating details of history seem sadly overlooked by some people there today—especially by the tourists and vacationers who flock to the many dude ranches. But the occasional frontier-day celebrations provide some reminders, even for those people.

Winter in Sterling County (page 99)

Several years ago Humble sent me out for some picture work in a new field near Sterling City, northwest of San Angelo. I drove over newly built sandy roads—and right into this snow scene. The winter sky, the thin white wintry blanket that in places scarcely covered the brown soil, and the lone oil pump enchanted me into doing this painting.

Old Trinity University at Tehuacana (page 100)

You can sometimes glimpse this old building far off to the left of the road (if you know where to look) when you approach Mexia from Waco along U.S. Highway 84. Originally it housed Trinity University, which opened its doors to students at what was then known as Tehuacana Springs on September 23, 1869. By 1890 Trinity boasted almost as many students as the town had inhabitants—three hundred to five hundred—and school officials began talking of moving to a larger place. Twelve years later they did move, to Waxahachie. In 1942 Trinity moved again, to its present location in San Antonio.

This unheralded but awe-inspiring edifice remains behind on Tehuacana Hill, a silent memorial to youths who studied there, graduated, established careers, and passed on. When I visited Tehuacana in 1961 the building still housed a school—Westminster University—but it had only a handful of students.

Old Dewberry House near Tyler (page 101)

Tyler is known for its roses—and rightly so. But some architecture of the vicinity also interests me—the Chilton Home, the LaGrande House, the Hambrick House a few miles out of town, and other places.

Seventeen miles southwest of Tyler, in the Teaselville community, stands this fine Old Dewberry House. It is the sole surviving two-story antebellum house in Smith County. The beautiful avenue of crape myrtle especially attracted me—and intrigued my host, Lee Lawrence, too. The height of those shrubs was fantastic. They were as tall as the house.

The residence, built by Colonel John Dewberry in 1854, is a large frame structure set on brick piers. The bricks used in the foundation and the chimneys were fired locally. Particular points of interest are a large downstairs hallway, which could be opened all the way through the house for ventilation, and window lights around the doorway. The front porch, with its massive wood colonnades and balustrades on the upper and lower levels, shows the predominant features of the Classic Revival Period.

The house was typical of large plantation homes. It was originally surrounded by outbuildings associated with the operation of the plantation. In front stood a large smokehouse, a cotton gin, and an office. The kitchen was separate from and to the rear of the house. Slave quarters, the carriage house, and several barns stood close by. A wing with several small rooms was added later, but this has been cut off and moved away.

Remnants of a formal garden can be seen between the house and the road. The deep shade afforded by the towering old cedar trees gives the house a ghostly appearance.

Colonel Dewberry, a Georgian, was one of the first white residents of the area now comprising Smith County. He was generally regarded as one of the wealthiest men living in the county before the Civil War. In an act of the First Legislature (in 1846) creating Smith County from a part of Nacogdoches County, Dewberry was named as one of five commissioners to locate a county seat to be known as Tyler. He died in 1877 and is buried southwest of the house in a masonry tomb.

Dewberry's stepdaughter, Mrs. Emma Loftin, inherited the plantation after his death. In 1908 it was purchased by the Edwards family. When I completed this picture members of that family still resided there.

The house was awarded the Historical Building Medallion by the state of Texas in 1963.

This picture is larger than most of my architectural subjects, since I wanted to include the avenue of crape myrtles broadside.

Captain Schreiner Home, Kerrville (page 102)

This ponderous old stone home in Kerrville was the residence of a remarkable man—Charles Armand Schreiner, born in France in 1838. He and his family moved to San Antonio in the 1850's, and at the age of sixteen he joined the Texas Rangers. Later he fought in the Civil War.

In 1869 he moved to Kerrville as a merchant. Business prospered. He became a banker and a rancher, and he made Kerrville the mohair capital of the world. He owned land stretching from Kerrville to Menard—a distance of eighty miles—but gave away much of his wealth, mainly to establish Schreiner Institute.

The original construction of this residence dates from the 1870's. Schreiner added the highly decorated front in the 1890's, when the house was extensively remodeled. After Schreiner's death in 1927 (at the age of eighty-eight) his residence was bought by the Masons.

Fredericksburg (page 103)

This approach might be described as working with symbols—or might be called a decorative pied. (I am poor at such designations.) I used Fredericksburg ingredients: windmills, blossoming fruit trees, the *kaffee mühle*, a goat fence at the extreme left.

The ominous black bars just got in somehow. This evolved during what I call my chaotic period, when I felt enmeshed in frustrations. But it is my favorite of that period.

William Pepper Cabin near Marble Falls (page 104)

About six miles out of Marble Falls I found the simple-styled William Pepper Cabin, which had remained amazingly intact for more than a century when I sketched it in 1962. In its two stories I found nearly all of the old cedar log work that went into the original construction so long ago.

Also in evidence was hardware hand-hammered from scrap iron.

Redbirds on the South Fork (page 105)

From my studio I could see the cypress trees putting on their fall wardrobe of gold and, all around, redbirds in abundance. The birds make an appearance at this time of year, and they are quick to find my bird feeders.

Actually this is another of my improvisations—I moved in some of the houses. But the redbirds are there right now —droves and droves of them—along with titmice and various breeds of sparrows. They all feel at home.

No. 506 Main Street, Old Log Cabin, Fredericksburg (page 106)

Typical of Hill Country construction is this use of rock and timber. The house itself—of log—is typical particularly of Fredericksburg, which has many structures remaining from the days of John Meusebach and the original German settlers. They came to Fredericksburg by wagon train from New Braunfels in 1846 and founded the community.

Scene on Lone Man Creek (page 107)

A request by Leon Jaworski to paint a scene for use on his Christmas card a few years ago brought me to this spot, a creek crossing on his picturesque place near Wimberley.

The horses and deer were genuine. During one visit I saw a deer come up to Leon's house for a handout. We fed him.

Aue House, Leon Springs (page 108)

Another view of this intriguing old house appeared in my first book. Max Aue, who came to Texas from Germany in 1850, built it, in well-designed Hill Country style.

Since I first saw the house—just off U.S. Highway 87 in

Leon Springs—I have driven by again and again. Every visit has shown me that it is falling apart at an alarming rate. Once I asked about renting the place—but was told it was not available. I wish I could buy and restore it myself. It would make ideal quarters for an artist.

Wilson County Courthouse, Floresville (page 109)

Wilson County and Floresville have an intriguing history. Many years ago the county lay in an area where Lipan Apaches, Comanches, and Tonkawas hunted. The town—or at least a place near it—was settled in the early 1830's by Don Francisco Flores de Abryo, a rancher. The coming of a railroad brought present Floresville into existence in 1885.

Despite the history, I feel now that I may not have done the subject justice. More movement, more life—maybe some local color like one of those horse trailers—might have helped in this picture.

The Alamo at Night (page 110)

I wanted to instill a feeling of drama in a picture of the Alamo, and I used this night approach. This is a dry-point etching, a medium I exploited in the early 1930's, in both architectural and marine scenes.

Judging by the reception, this etching attracted attention. I have had many calls for it. I had a batch of these proofs, but I don't know where they are now.

Fort McKavett Barracks (page 111)

This old army post in Menard County was originally established in 1852 for frontier protection and served for seven years before being abandoned. Around 1870 it was reopened—and rebuilt—and must have presented a bustling scene. After Indian raids ceased, the fort was again abandoned by the army, in the 1880's, this time permanently.

The cavalry no longer gallops out of here, but the place had not been entirely abandoned when I painted it in 1961. Living in the barracks then were numerous Mexican American families who had reinforced the roofs with some colorful, impromptu materials—rugs, asbestos, tin. Still, I exaggerated the colors in this picture—and I moved onto the scene the ruins of an old chimney. (I don't pull any punches when I try to make what you would call an "adequate picture" out of a composition.)

You might notice how sky and earth colors blend. Instead of painting the stereotyped blue sky of Texas I wanted to give the feeling of this particular western scene.

Scene on San Antonio River (page 112)

The river that winds through the heart of San Antonio brings the city picturesqueness. Springs rising just north of San Antonio give the river its impetus and keep it flowing in a more constant volume than most other Texas streams.

This peculiarity also brought the town into being in the first place and made it an important locale. In 1691 Spaniards on a tour into East Texas to inspect, establish, and strengthen missions there found an Indian village on the river banks around the present site of San Antonio. They named the river and the village San Antonio de Padua. Eighteen years later Father Antonio Olivares came upon the cool river and the surrounding green valley and was so charmed by the scene that he wanted to establish a mission there. He did, in 1718, and the town of San Antonio was born.

My own visit to the river and the ensuing sketch were made in 1924, when I was concentrating on pencil work.

Kyser Ruins, Cherry Spring (page 113)

These old buildings at Cherry Spring fascinated me. I drove up to the place two or three times before I could get in. Each time I found the gate locked and nobody around.

Climbing over the fence or the gate would have been simple, but I refrained from making so blatant an entry.

Finally, on a Sunday in April, some people appeared—descendants of earlier owners. They had come down from Fort Worth to visit what is known as the old Kyser place, and they were glad to show me around. The home and barn groups, both of worthwhile architecture, seemed relegated to oblivion. I was intrigued by the barn—the log and stone wings with slits for rifles to ward off Indian attacks. Wild flowers grew in profusion.

Many Chimneys, Old San Antonio (page 114)

The chimneys in this old San Antonio home fascinated me. I sketched the house in 1926 and do not know whether it still stands, or where.

Wherever it stood, those chimneys and the slanted roof are reminiscent of many houses I saw in an old section of San Antonio known as the Irish Flat. The Mexican War (1846–1848) first brought the Irish to San Antonio—as U.S. Army sutlers and teamsters. Because they worked mostly at the Alamo, which had become a center of Quartermaster's activity then, they settled on a small area of vacant land nearby. Their community thrived for decades after that, but hardly any vestige remains now.

Irish Flat (page 115)

A manufacturer asked me to try this painting—done with his colored inks—to see how his product would work when used as a wash and how permanent it would be.

I enjoyed the experiment—but found that the inks were not absolutely permanent. Sunlight affected them. They had to be kept in the shade to prevent their fading badly.

A Visit to the Alamo (page 116)

I feel certain that I have pictured the Alamo at least

twenty-five times. This is one scene—and one phase of my work: the Alamo, with human and animal figures, drawn for *The Texas Sketchbook*.

The Alamo as known today is much more significant for its history than for its architecture. The building that stands restored in downtown San Antonio is the church, which was originally only a small part of a compound that sprawled over more than four acres of land. At the time of the 1836 battle strong stone walls enclosed the compound (except for a space in front of the church) and encompassed barracks, officers' quarters, a hospital, pens for animals, and other areas.

After the battle the Alamo lay in ruins for years. In the 1850's the U.S. Army restored it for use as a Quartermaster's depot to store grain and hay. (Rebuilt would be a better word to use here, because the restoration was haphazard at best.) In 1883—forty-seven years after the tragic fall—the state of Texas bought the building and began to take some interest in preserving it.

I am always reluctant to sketch the Alamo. Perhaps it is too much of a challenge, or perhaps (as I mentioned in my first book) it is better portrayed in words than in drawings or paintings.

Bedding Down (page 117)

Here is a cold-weather scene from out of the past: humped Brahman cattle hovering around a gas flare in an oil field near Webster, in southern Harris County, trying to get what warmth they can.

Decades ago gas flares were plentiful, but after World War II a gas conservation program was begun. Today a scattering of oil storage tanks across farms and ranches usually is the only clue to the existence of an oil field in the area.

The cattle deserve a note. Brahmans, a breed from India, were introduced into Texas shortly before 1900. You can see many of them along the coast. They are hardy animals—able to take high temperatures and to resist the onslaught of pests like ticks and mosquitoes.

Mission Concepción, San Antonio (page 118)

My favorite mission in San Antonio is Concepción, and a note in my first book told why. I shall simply repeat it here:

Whereas Mission San José overwhelms you with its magnitude and its discreet use of Spanish Renaissance ornamentation, Mission Concepción satisfies with its pure line and design, its flawless and almost brazen simplicity.

Another view of Concepción appears on page 126.

On the Wareing Place (page 119)

A wonderful mixture of rock work and timber went into the construction of this old homestead near Fredericksburg. It is one of the most charming sights in the Hill Country. Everything about it falls into place beautifully, even with the use of those different building materials.

The house had a magnificent cellar still stocked with jars of preserves someone had put up long ago—maybe half a century earlier—and had forgotten. I took one jar home, tasted the contents, and found the preserves still good to eat after all that time.

Another view of the place appears on page 125—*Remnants of a Ranch near Fredericksburg.*

Scene on San Antonio River (page 120)

This picture resembles in style the one on page 112, but this was done three years earlier, while I was at Texas A&M. I visited San Antonio that year—1921—when I was going in heavily for pencil work, experimenting and copying drawings. During the visit I made several sketches around the city—not many.

Look at the foliage in the picture. It is a wiggly sort of thing, typical of my trees and shrubs at that time.

Early Winter on the Guadalupe (page 121)

See that blue heron? People often have asked, "What's it doing up here on this river?" Usually those birds prefer salt water.

But I did not improvise the heron. It belongs in this scene. Every evening before sunset, for years and years, that huge bird would fly up and down the river—and flap by our place each time.

This scene depicts the turn of fall near Camp Mystic on the South Fork. The flaming red bushes would have told you the time of year even if I had not.

As I write this I am engaged in working on a large oil painting of the scene, but so far it has not come off well. My first attempt at putting down a picture—done while I am captivated by a feeling—usually is more spontaneous and more successful. That seems to be true in this case. When I try to rework I suddenly get conscious of structure and other technicalities and try to get too much into the picture.

San Fernando Cathedral, San Antonio (page 122)

I sketched this view of San Fernando Cathedral fifty years ago, looking from the rear of the building toward the front. The romantic aura, the rich heritage, and the architecture of many of these old San Antonio buildings continue to excite me. This simplified French Gothic cathedral was constructed on the site of the old San Fernando parish church, where General Santa Anna unfurled his blood-red "no-quarter" flag for the men of the Alamo to see on the afternoon of February 23, 1836.

The cornerstone of the original church was laid in 1738, but it was not completed until twenty years later. Construction of the present edifice began in 1868—encompassing the old structure so neatly that services continued to be held there as work progressed. Four years later, with the new construction nearly finished, workmen demolished the old church dome that had witnessed the unfurling of Santa Anna's terrible flag.

Old Barns near Center Point (page 123)

The simplicity of this scene on the road between Center Point and Kerrville attracted me. The goats were there, but I added the chickens to get a typical Hill Country rural view.

Of interest to me also was the weathervane. You still see some vanes like it in the area, particularly around Luckenbach, in Gillespie County.

Excerpts from Fredericksburg Cemetery (page 124)

Most of the names on these tombstones are German.

Many of the people who lie buried here carved out a community from Indian frontier. Through the exercise of wisdom they succeeded admirably. In the spring of 1847 their leader, John Meusebach, made a treaty with the Comanches that brought lasting peace—in contrast to other communities where bloody conflicts raged for years.

The windmills, water tanks, and stone house are typical of Fredericksburg. Iron work around some of the graves has been sketched to show detail. The cherub's head drawn at lower right pictures one of Elisabet Ney's last pieces of sculpture.

Remnants of a Ranch near Fredericksburg (page 125)

This fine item of indigenous Gillespie County architecture and its adroit use of materials enthralled me. Mrs. John Staub insisted that I see it, and she drove me to it over a dirt road leading off from State Highway 16 that goes to Llano. The place so fascinated me that I have two paintings of it in this book. The other one appears on page 119.

The barn struck me as being a real gem. Inside it I saw some wonderful hand-hewn cypress beams.

Some people think I overdid myself with the size of that tree, but I did not. It really was tall and magnificent. I did exercise some artistic license elsewhere, by restoring the original shingles to part of that roof. I also fussed with Bill Wareing (of Houston), the owner of this place, about his tearing down an old outside stairway (not seen in the picture). Now I think he has decided to restore it, along with the entire homestead.

John Staub told me something about the history of the place. It was built by the Kiehne family, whose ancestral lineage was brought from Germany to Fredericksburg by Frederick Kiehne, founder of an early blacksmith shop on the town's Main Street. There the striving smithy catered to United States cavalrymen, '49'ers on their way to California, and even Indians, who liked to stand around and watch the work, fascinated by the fire, bellows, and anvils.

In 1850 Frederick Kiehne built near his shop the first two-story limestone residence constructed in Fredericksburg In the late 1850's he and his sons, Frederick, Jr., and William, acquired the land on which this homestead later was built.

Mission Concepción, San Antonio (page 126)

As I have indicated in my comment on the Mission Concepción picture on page 118, I am less impressed with the ornateness of Mission San José and its Rose Window than I am with the scale and sheer simplicity of Concepción. This is *the* mission, I think—and O'Neil Ford, the San Antonio architect, shares this feeling with me. The doorway pictured here is one of the most beautifully scaled items I have seen in any of the missions.

This picture dates from my etching period, which began in the 1920's at the Art Students' League. There I learned the fundamentals, the techniques.

Etching is a difficult medium—a forgotten one, too. Getting the inks on paper without smudging the whole picture is a tricky operation.

Terlingua (page 127)

This marvelous chimney in the crumbling old quicksilver mining town of Terlingua, near Big Bend National Park, was the only subject of any consequence to paint here, but it made the picture—that one vertical projection.

I took this particular trip to the Big Bend in 1948 with a company writer in search of material for an article in *The Humble Way*. A blizzard left us snowbound in a lodging for a while, but after the weather thawed we left our hibernation and made this trek to old Terlingua.

The town acquired its name from nearby Terlingua Creek. Some people in the vicinity claim that "Terlingua" means "three languages": Spanish, English, and "Texan." The first settlers in the country, Mexican herders, had to contend with Apache, Comanche, and Shawnee Indians who roamed the Big Bend wilderness. Not until the early 1890's, when the mercury mining began, did a permanent community develop here. Quicksilver worth $3 million soon was recovered from the Chisos Mine, named after the surrounding mountains. Shortly after World War II water flooded the shafts —about the same time that quicksilver prices fell—and the one-time boom town of Terlingua faded into history. The laborers, offered anything they could use when the mining ceased, tore out ceiling timbers, window frames, doors, and even the roof and the front of an adobe theater. They took all this material with them, along with their personal possessions, which explains adobe Terlingua's sudden return toward dust.

View of Eagle Pass (page 128)

The Mexican border scene always has delighted me since Pop Mabry of Humble and I used to "ride the boards"—check poster locations—as part of our advertising chores in the 1930's. The posters always seemed to be in the worst possible shape in the vicinity of the border. At least that's where we usually headed first when sent out on this work. The life and color of Piedras Negras, Nuevo Laredo, and other Mexican towns just happened to be nearby.

At Eagle Pass (across from Piedras Negras) this store front intrigued me because it smacked of Mexico. It was located in Texas, of course, near the river, but it seemed to belong on the opposite side.

Other people ride the boards now—and they can have the chore. Increased showings and a terror about time and deadlines have ruined the job. I try to keep modern in other ways. I subscribe to a number of publications, see many shows, try to acquire new experiences. I like to study new movements, new views—in art and outside of it.

As I said earlier in these comments, I am still a student. In my own work I often feel that I have not scratched the surface yet. I have many plans and projects.